REAL ESTATE SALES IN A NUTSHELL...

Is it Right for You?

By Joe Cobb

Real Estate Sales in a Nutshell

Do Something Today That Your Future Self Will Thank You For

Copyright © 2014 Joe Cobb

All rights reserved.

ISBN-10: 1503237982
ISBN-13: 978-1503237988

"When You Want To Be the Best ….Only an Expert Will Do!"

This book is for you!

If you are considering a career in real estate sales (or have perhaps entered the profession and are struggling now to make up your mind whether you should stay or seek a different means for your livelihood), you should find this book of TREMENDOUS value, aid and assistance. It will help you to know "in a nutshell" the fundamentals of what you'll need to do and what you'll need to know – in order to be a successful professional in real estate sales.

"Refreshingly straight talk about a career in real estate sales by a true expert."   ---by **Marty Judge, Immediate Past President Rancho Bernardo Business Association.**

"Every page, every chapter in this little book of real estate wisdom is a must read for all real estate agents. I asked myself, Anil Mavalankar, how come YOU did not think of that? Do not be fooled by the size of this book. It is packed with common sense practical tools. It has the road map of ideas, wisdom and years of experience all-in one little book. Joe Cobb makes this book of success, a simple step-by-step recipe for all real estate agents. This book reveals the degree of knowledge and wisdom rarely seen in the real estate business. It is a joy to read this book."   ---by **Anil Mavalankar, Real Estate Broker Associate for thirty two years.**

Real Estate Sales in a Nutshell

> "You Are Never Too Old To Set Another Goal Or To Dream A New Dream."
>
> -C.S. Lewis

"When You Want To Be the Best ….Only an Expert Will Do!"

About the Author

Joe began his career as a REALTOR® in 1975. He obtained his Brokers License in 1978 and has earned the National Association of REALTORS® designations of GRI, Graduate of REALTORS® Institute, and E-Pro which is specific training on the use of the internet and related technology for marketing and communication.

Over the years he has managed or owned several national franchises. He now runs a successful multi-office real estate brokerage in San Diego in its 22nd year with over 80 real estate agents and brokers. He is most involved with his agents as trainer, coach, mentor, counselor and problem solver.

Through their firm's Training Academy, they provide in-depth training for sales agent licensing and preparation for a successful career in real estate.

You can reach Joe at 858-967-8801 by calling or texting or email him at JoeCobb@RealtyExperts.Net. He is also on Facebook and LinkedIn. He will be glad to meet with you to help you further decide on this career opportunity.

Real Estate Sales in a Nutshell

> *It's Not How Good You Are*
> *It's*
> *How Good You Want To Be*

"When You Want To Be the Best ….Only an Expert Will Do!"

CONTENTS

	Why I wrote this book	Pg. 9
1	HOW I BROKE INTO REAL ESTATE SALES	Pg. 11
2	IT STARTS WITH YOU	Pg. 17
3	YOUR COMMITMENTS	Pg. 31
4	FREEDOM?	Pg. 37
5	EFFECTIVE TIME MANAGEMENT	Pg. 43
6	PROSPECTING AND MARKETING	Pg. 49
7	QUALIFYING ALL THE TIME	Pg. 57
8	PRESENTING	Pg. 65
9	MENTORING YOUR CLIENTS	Pg. 71
10	BUILDING A BUSINESS FOR LIFE	Pg. 79
11	TECHNOLOGY AND R. E. SALES	Pg. 89
12	THOUGHTS, TIPS AND MYTHS	Pg. 93
13	BEYOND RESIDENTIAL REAL ESTATE	Pg. 101
14	REVIEW OF WHAT YOU LEARNED	Pg. 105
15	IS REAL ESTATE SALES RIGHT FOR YOU	Pg. 109
	More About the Author	Pg. 115

DEDICATION

This book is dedicated to the future agents who hopefully will have a better chance of success as a result of reading this book.

ACKNOWLEDGEMENTS

To all of the people who have been a part of my life. Those from whom I have learned as well as those it has been my pleasure to assist in their career. I offer my thanks to each and every one of you for challenging me to be better and better every day.

To my family. A special thanks to the ones who have had to put up with their father in the roll of "boss" in one or more of my business ventures. I hope this book may be useful to you as well. I thank David Kellough, my brother-in-law who edited the first draft and inspired me to go forward. I am especially thankful to my wife Paula who read and re-read my many proofs and helped me make this book much easier to read and what it is today.

To my friends who contributed thoughts and expertise with their in depth editing and suggestions. Especially Authors Marty Judge, Richard Villasana and Amazon river Author Mynor Schult.

"When You Want To Be the Best ….Only an Expert Will Do!"

Why I wrote this book.

In the past thirty–five years, I have known too many people who initially got into the real estate business thinking it is a "slam dunk" job. They went into it with the impression that all you have to do is drive around with your friends, look at houses, go to escrow, and pick up a check. LOOK at that BIG CHECK!!

Now that might work for one or two sales to your closest friends or family who may have encouraged you to get your license. But then what do you do? What about future sales? You need more than one or two sales to actually make a decent, long – term living.

Truth is, real estate sales is hard work! There are a great many things you must know and do in order to be successful. Statistics show the vast majority of all agents leave the business within two to three years, simply because they misjudged the degree of work and discipline necessary to learn the key principles required for success.

So you ask, "What is the difference between those who leave the business and those who stay and make a good living?" That is the reason for this book.

I have created this guide to help you see what it takes and to determine if a real estate career is a good choice for you.

I have written the first chapters using residential real estate examples to introduce the basics of real estate sales.

Chapter 13 expands on the basics to look at the whole field of real estate opportunities you can consider as a career path.

This book is not an exhaustive text on how to be a real estate broker or salesperson. It is, however, an introduction to some of the most important elements of a successful real estate career.

> *Nobody Said That It'd Be Easy...*
> *They Just Promised It Would Be Worth It*

> *If You Want Something You've Never Had Then You've Got To Do Something You've Never Done*

Chapter One

HOW I BROKE INTO REAL ESTATE SALES AS A CAREER

How I Broke into Real Estate Sales as a Career

The Difference Between The Impossible And The Possible Lies In a Person's Determination

"When You Want To Be the Best ….Only an Expert Will Do!"

Here is how I broke into real estate sales as a career: I married my first wife, Diane in 1966. By early 1968 we had our first child and were living in an apartment in Los Angeles. I was busy running a business, and all of a sudden Diane told me we had to buy a home for our family. I told her we could not afford it, and I had no money for a down payment and did not see how we could take on the debt for a mortgage. She was not bringing in a paycheck so, of course, I figured that was the end of it.

The next thing I knew she had found this hotshot real estate lady who was very good, and she was showing me these homes she found for us. Not knowing how to firmly say no to my new wife and mother of my child, I went along with the program and put in an offer on one for the great sum of $28,500 which included a good amount of furniture and had a fantastic 180 degree hilltop view from the top of Mt. Washington. It was just the right home for this "successful young entrepreneur." Great on the ego! She caught me in just the right moment when the business was in a good cash position. The truth was we really did not have the money for the down payment by the time the escrow was to close. Her strong desire for the home and my unstoppable attitude made it all happen. I simply did what it took to find the money that was needed. I got on the phone and called all the people including those I had no reason to believe would have the money until I found it. I almost fell off my chair when my sister said she would lend it to us. So that was a case of sheer willpower on the part of my wife and I to make it happen. She was determined and I was motivated to make it happen once the decision had been made. Motivation and determination by you and your clients is the glue that makes success possible.

A fast forward five more years found us in San Diego renting a house again with three kids and the same situation happens again. We had moved and had tenants in the home in Los Angeles. Diane said, "I want to live in a home we own." I said, "We cannot afford it, and we have no money for a down." Besides that I told her we could only buy in this better neighborhood, and we cannot afford that area at all. Yep, she found another hotshot real estate broker who was very good with creative financing, and he did the loan and the sale and carried his commission (we made payments to him after closing). And, yes, I had to scramble to find our closing costs and succeeded again. We purchased that home for $32,000 and sold it five years later for $78,000. At the time we purchased that home I was making just $129 per week at a fifty five hour a week job. It was her adamant will to buy and my desire and action to get that house after she found it that made it happen! That home had netted us $800 every month for the time we owned it! I was hooked on real estate!!

It took me a year after studying for my license to really start selling. I maintained my 55 hour a week job at the San Diego Union from early in the morning to 10:30 a.m. as District Distribution Manager overseeing paperboys and girls delivering routes in Pacific Beach. I got home, took a nap, and went to the office to sell real estate in the afternoons and evenings. It was very tiring, and I had little sleep but soon became the top sales person in the office of 24 agents. It was very scary to quit the regular paying job to go full time in real estate, but I did and succeeded. It was tough at times as the economy and interest rates fluctuated, but I would never look back. It has been fun, rewarding, and worth getting into. I had found my passion.

> *The Only Way To Do Great Work Is To Love What You Do*
>
> *Steve Jobs*

How I Broke into Real Estate Sales as a Career

> *If You Don't Go After What You Want You'll Never Have It. If You Don't Ask The Answer Is Always No. If You Don't Step Forward You're Always In The Same Place*

Chapter Two

IT STARTS WITH YOU

It Starts With You

{
Follow Your Heart
Live Your Dream
Be Passionate
Happiness Is Yours To Take
Never Give Up
Your Energy Is Limitless
Embrace Possibility
Love Your Life
}

"When You Want To Be the Best ….Only an Expert Will Do!"

It starts with who you are. As a REALTOR®, how you relate to potential clients and situations is influenced by your background, your self-confidence, your opinion of others and how you see the world around you.

Make no mistake, real estate is a *people business*. It has to do with your particular ability to relate to others and understand how they feel. It is about asking the right questions and listening to each individual in the transaction. Your job is to make a connection with them in order to find that house or property that can fulfill their needs and desires or know how to promote their home or property for sale.

People like working with someone with whom they can relate and make a connection. So here are a few detailed questions to ask yourself as you think about your future career. Your answers may be the key to whom you may seek to work within your career.

Where were you raised? In the city? A small town? A farm? Did you grow up in the South, North, East, or West? Were you born or raised in a different country? You may find people who come from any of these places will be very receptive to you.

What languages do you speak? Were you in the military? Did you go to college? Did you obtain a degree? If so, what degree? Are you religious? Your connection and common ground can be the reason your prospects work with

It Starts With You

you. Most people like people who they can relate to on many levels.

Do other people intimidate you? Do you see a purpose in your life? Do you believe in honest and ethical behavior? Do you enjoy helping people? Do you have a passion and belief in the value of people owning their own home? Do you see the value of real estate vs stocks and bonds? Do you believe the value found in real estate is a better method of building your estate? Are you a good listener? Do you see the value and necessity for compromise in order to obtain what you want?

Your answer to these and the following questions may be what either propels you to success or holds you back.

What are your fears, your hopes and your dreams? How do you perceive your attitude about life? Is your glass half full or half empty?

Very importantly, what is your passion? What would you want to do if you did not have to work in order to make an income?

I have come to believe it takes a passion for real estate in order to really be successful. If you have that and seek the right set of skills, abilities and knowledge, money comes as your reward.

Through the years I have met many people who, when I asked what their passion is, answered with anything but sell real estate. Yet, ironically, that was what they were trying to do.

"When You Want To Be the Best ….Only an Expert Will Do!"

They often said they would go for their passion only after they made a lot of money. These people missed the point. Without passion they fail to make that money, and as a result, they typically wind up leaving the business with limited success.

Besides passion and the right set of skills, abilities and knowledge, quite frequently selling real estate also requires thick skin and perseverance to confront difficult obstacles. You must have total confidence and full-blown optimism to overcome what is often the inevitable. Your friends and relatives use another agent to buy or sell their home. The home your clients love gets sold to someone else, just as they decide to make an offer. The home they choose gets an inspection that reveals too much work is required, and the seller may refuse to fix it. Just as your buyers find the home of their dreams their car dies, and they have to buy another one with financing that makes it impossible to qualify for the new mortgage on the home they want. Someone becomes ill or loses their job while in escrow. You work with buyers, and interest rates go up kicking them out of the market. The home does not appraise, and the buyers or sellers won't compromise. A third party, relative or friend talks your clients out of a sale or talks them into using another agent after you have spent hours with them.

The wasted time and the gas money spent driving buyers around who do not buy can be extremely frustrating. All such things have the potential to overwhelm and discourage an agent.

I had several of these experiences and became very frustrated each time. The one that stands out above them all

It Starts With You

was when a new pastor of my church was looking for a home. I was happily focusing on my investment real estate business. I had been very successful in residential sales and very visible to the congregation of 1,600 people. The new pastor's wife was told I was the best agent to work with to find their home. So she called me up, said she knew my reputation, and wanted only me to help her. I told her I would rather not because of my investment business, and it would take me some time to adapt to her wishes in order to do a good job for her. I also told her I needed both her and her husband to meet with me to affirm they were both committed to the process so that (of course) I would be paid for my time. She insisted I help her and that she had to be the only one to meet with me because her husband was too busy taking over his duties at my church. He had told her he would go along with her no matter what. She was very friendly but insistent on my helping her. That all sounded logical and acceptable because I could count on the pastor and his wife to treat me right. Right? I told her I had a family to support and must know for sure she would work only with me and any time they saw a home that interested them to call me so I could serve them by helping them see and purchase it.

It was a buyer's market with many homes to see so I spent considerable time with her showing homes and working through those available. She had given me the commitment. He personally had not.

After hours of working with her, I found out her husband had found a house and they purchased it from another Realtor he had run across who once was in his congregation at another church. That really hurt, especially because she had insisted on using me and PROMISED they would buy through me if I would take my valuable time from my investment company to help her. Those were promises broken, commitments ignored, and no pay for valuable time spent. I was very, very surprised and hurt!

Another time I found a young man about my age who wanted to buy a house. He said he finally decided to settle down and wanted a home for his future wife and him to enjoy. I asked if he had someone in mind, and he responded "yes," but it was early in their relationship but she looked like she could be the one. I then said, "Ok, let's include her in the search so we find the home that fits her as well." No, he said because he was the one who would buy it whether he marries her or not. He then promised I would be his agent for the purchase no matter what.

It was another buyer's market, and he was not sure where he wanted to live so I spent many hours and days showing him homes in different areas over a period of weeks. By then we really became close friends during which time he became engaged. Then when we finally narrowed our search to a nice area, he told me he had to concentrate for the next two weeks on his bride and planning for their wedding in two or three months. I told him we could then get his future wife in on our search.

This time it was the bride's mother who knew a great Realtor. So the next thing I knew this guy came in excited to tell me they found their house. He was actually forgetting our first qualifying questions I had asked, including his commitment to me as his Realtor. He was only thinking of me as his FRIEND! I was really upset at him, and I let him know in words I soon wanted to take back because I had seen him as a friend too. I had asked the right questions and received the right answers at the time but trusted his words of commitment. I was devastated again, and it took a long time to get over it. Most importantly I felt guilty for what I said and swore not to let that happen again.

That was a breakthrough experience for me. I learned to rejoice in the joy of my friends and relatives and wish them well even when they buy or sell their homes when I thought they should be committed to me. I have found peace from this approach. Now I say "on to the next" with no remorse. I know now to keep asking the right questions and reminding clients of, and confirming their commitment. It rarely happens anymore.

The good news is, you will learn to minimize all of this, and I will explore many of the means of doing so in subsequent chapters.

What do you expect to get out of selling real estate? Is it freedom? Quick and easy money? Fulfillment? More time off? Maybe even being your own boss? It may be any of these things, but a feeling of fulfillment should be high up on your list. You should be someone who gets the feeling of fulfillment when you help clients (who often times become your good friends) to realize their dreams and find the home or property

"When You Want To Be the Best ….Only an Expert Will Do!"

they desire or help them sell their property for a fair and equitable price. When the sale closes and you finally do get paid, you usually forget the challenges you overcame to get there. Your friends are happy and you have earned a living.

How do you see yourself actually working on selling real estate every day? What do you think successful agents do? Too many people get into the field without realizing the obvious. It is a *sales* job, and you are actually expected to *sell*. Not only that, but people are paying you a lot of money, in the form of commissions, which is one of the reasons you are considering a career as a real estate *sales* agent, right?

The vast majority of agents get into real estate thinking they do not have to sell. When they find out they cannot make a living without putting in the work by calling and talking to people and knocking on doors, they leave the business.

Without a passion for helping people buy and sell real estate, looking for people to help may seem frightening or overwhelming. To be happy in real estate you must be confident and competent. You have to know that you are the best choice for anybody who needs an agent.

The focus on making money removes you from the true focus of a great salesperson. Finding what the client wants and helping them get it should be your primary goal. You must have passion within your heart to find people to help every day because it is a numbers game. The more people you

It Starts With You

communicate with, the more likely you will find someone ready, willing and able to buy or sell real estate.

The truth is, without the structure of a real job, many agents do not work productively. They sell only the homes that fall in their lap.

Why do you want to be a real estate agent? Think quickly. On a scale of one to ten (with ten being the highest) what is your motivation to be a real estate sales agent? The motivation for many is *money,* and, with passion, once you have developed and honed your real estate sales skills, you can indeed earn a high income with a great lifestyle and the flexibility to do more than you could at most other jobs.

Your goal may be to use the money to help someone else or to get a better home for yourself or your family; to invest in real estate; to donate to a good cause; to provide money for your kids' college education, or to help your family in still other ways. Your goal can be anything, but it should include the pure joy of helping people find the home or property they desire and gaining new friends. If your motivation to do so is not a seven or above on this scale, you need to really think about doing something else.

As I said before, it is the *passion* that makes the difference. So after you finish this book and know more about what's required in the job, you should ask yourself if you have the passion that is required.

When do you want to start your new career? The answer to this question often comes as a surprise to those thinking of real estate sales. Too often they think they can get their license quickly, jump right in and start earning huge commissions immediately.

They also often believe they could do a much better job than others they have seen and do so right away. (True, perhaps some could, because our industry does have its share of incompetent agents out there. But there is way too much to learn to do an EXPERT job quickly!)

This thinking is best summed up by the saying on our Training Academy wall:

Four levels of (real estate) expertise:

1.　New untrained agents are "Unconsciously Incompetent." (They do not know what they do not know!)

2.　They are "Consciously Incompetent." (They know they do not know what they should.)

3.　They are "Consciously Competent." (They practice what to say, how to say it, and have check lists to make sure they do everything right.)

4.　They are "Unconsciously Competent." (They know what to do and how to do it without having to actively think about it. They have everything memorized so it becomes automatic. Nevertheless, they still have to practice their skills and follow established checklists of all the items that are essential in working with every client.)

To get to the third and fourth levels should be your immediate goal. However, there is a GREAT DEAL to learn. It takes time with numerous classes, seminars and lots of coaching to get there. You must change your old habits into new and productive habits. Your first year or two could be somewhat slow. However, with passion, motivation, the right skill set and coaching, you improve your chances for more rapid success.

Another surprise for many is how long the process takes for getting licensed and making any money. Typically licensing takes three to four months or more, depending on your focus and ability to pass the State test the first time. In California you have to take two mandatory classes and one additional class of your choice. Each class takes no less than 18 days. Then you can apply for the test and wait sometimes for three to four weeks for your test date. After you pass the test and undergo a thorough background check, you may apply for your real estate license. At this point you have a fairly good idea what real estate is as well as the laws and practices expected of you by your State. However, this is when your *true* education in real estate *sales* begins. Now you start what is, in reality, a life-long learning process – studying and attending still more classes and seminars to advance and improve your knowledge, your skills, your habits and your career. And as you know from my examples so far, experience is one of the main ways we learn. Even today I am running across issues I have not seen before.

"When You Want To Be the Best ….Only an Expert Will Do!"

Bottom line is, unless you are highly unusual, you are unlikely to have much money coming in during your first six months. Fact is, you have to spend money to get into the real estate business. Your financial obligation includes schooling, licensing, association dues, multiple listing fees, signs, business cards and other basic costs of doing business. More expenses include computers, iPads, smartphones and marketing expenses. A fair estimate may amount to $2,000, $3,000 or more. This is *before* you have any income.

Reality also sets in when you learn that the huge commission you charge for your services gets split 50/50 between the Broker you work for and the cooperating Broker. (There are two sides to every transaction, a listing and a selling side.) But then, you have to split *your* commission side with your *Broker*. When I first got my license, I quickly learned the 6% commission I was to charge meant I would receive only 1½% from the entire commission. That's quite a significant difference!

Many people start on the path to a long-term career in real estate but fall by the wayside for lack of income. In fact, many licensed agents do not have more than one or two sales their first year. It is your level of *commitment* and *passion*, as well as the guidance of your Broker, Trainer and Coach, that will determine your level of success.

It Starts With You

> *"We Can Complain Because Rose Bushes Have Thorns, Or Rejoice Because Thorn Bushes Have Roses"*
>
> *-Abraham Lincoln*

Chapter Three

YOUR COMMITMENTS

Your Commitments

> *"There's A Difference Between Interest And Commitment*
>
> *When You're Interested In Doing Something, You Do It Only When It's Convenient.*
>
> *When You're Committed To Something, You Accept No Excuses; Only Results"*
>
> *-Kenneth Blanchard*

Commitment to your career. In most fields of endeavor there are professional organizations that promote high competency and ethical standards. They establish systems, classes, publications, seminars, etc., all aimed at raising the level of expertise in their industry. The real estate field is no exception. We have long–established national, state and local associations, all dedicated to giving you the information and tools to assist you in the success of your career.

I would NEVER suggest that you consider working for a broker who is not a member of the National Association of REALTORS® (NAR). There is simply too much to learn, and your best way of learning and keeping up with laws and current real estate news and practices is by joining the association. When you do so (and *maintain* your membership), you are an on-going REALTOR®. The title "REALTOR®" is trademarked and may NOT be used unless you continue to be a member of the NAR. So for the sake of your clients and for a successful career, you must commit to always be a member.

You should also plan to take advantage of all of the associations' seminars and classes held locally and nationally in order to learn all you can. Being active in the running of the association is a step you could also consider, in order to learn more about your chosen career while you associate with other career REALTORS® and learn how they practice real estate. A newer agent may do it to learn while an experienced REALTOR® does it to improve their association.

Your Commitments

In any case, you must be committed to doing an EXPERT job and committed to real estate as a long-term career in order to succeed. Those who think they can make a quick buck and go on to something else do not understand the importance of being in business for yourself and all that entails. You are in charge of getting your leads and converting them to customers. You get paid for finding or selling their homes only after you get an escrow closed.

Remember those four levels of competence? Again, you must be committed to learning all of the skills and systems it takes to give EXPERT service. And you must be committed to providing it over and over again.

A real estate career is never stagnant. It requires practice and continual learning of the newest and latest in the field for the rest of your life. An old saying is, "The day you decide you know it all and don't need to learn anymore, is the day you might as well climb into a coffin and wait!" This saying applies no matter who you are or what job you have.

Commitment to your clients. You MUST also be committed to the best interest of your clients even when it may mean you do not make an immediate sale or receive the immediate income from it as a result. For example, it might be easy not to mention an important issue your client should be aware of in order to close the sale. On one occasion I learned of an agent who told a client not to worry about a termite report and did not even show the report to the client until after the close of escrow. That did not end well. The agent lost his job, and the Broker involved felt morally obligated (that was me) to spend thousands of dollars to do the work required by the termite report. Always remember that any lies and falsehoods can only end up giving you a bad reputation, which is death to any agent and the broker he or she works for. You will learn that your reputation is everything, and by committing to always doing an honest, EXPERT job, you set yourself up for repeat clients and business referrals in the future.

The good news is people move (often two or three times in a ten year period). Plus, people often like to brag to their friends and family about their great REALTOR® and the terrific job he or she did. Invariably their friends and family move too and often want to use that same great REALTOR® to help them. I have had one of my agents count 24 sales over 12 years, just from *one* new satisfied client! She was their REALTOR® of choice. Obviously she was a very successful REALTOR® over a long career!

Your Commitments

> "Success Seems To Be Connected With Action.
> Successful People Keep Moving.
> They Make Mistakes, But They Don't Quit."
>
> -Conrad Hilton

Chapter Four

FREEDOM?

Freedom?

> "Ability Is What You're Capable Of Doing.
>
> Motivation Determines What You Do.
>
> Attitude Determines How Well You Do It."
>
> -Lou Holtz

Freedom? Your worst boss? Or your best boss? Okay, so you quit your job to become a real estate agent. You can now choose your own hours and do whatever you want, seven days a week, right? No more alarms or watching the clock. No more time cards or bosses telling you what to do. You've got complete freedom! Right?

OOPS! Wait a minute! Now *you* have to exercise self-discipline, be your own boss, make your own schedule and hold yourself accountable in order to make any money. The big question is, when do you come to that full realization? Some agents never get to that point where they invoke a strict set of tasks and things to do for their work days, utilizing good time management. Instead, they go to the office and *look* busy, getting ready to get started to begin to prospect. Of course, the conversations at the office seem to be useful for education or to keep up with what is going on. The agent meetings and caravans to see houses are fun. The refreshments are always good. But, the time flies by with little to show for it. Before you know it, it's time to go home for dinner, and you haven't accomplished a thing!

Oh, but you can work at home, too! Right? You can work just as soon as you take the clothes out of the dryer, or finish watering the yard, or just pick up something at the store, clean the car, go shopping for a few things, or fix dinner. "I will get to that prospecting, or calling for that listing appointment just as soon as I get this or that other thing done."

Freedom?

For me, it is the refrigerator that keeps calling from the kitchen. Every time I work from home that happens, and I gain weight. Some things are just easier done at the office just so long as others are not too distracting.

Ah, but then when the bills stack up, that's when you get a check, but it's a *reality check*! You HAVE to do what you HAVE to do, *not* necessarily what you WANT to do. NOW you have a boss again, but it's an even worse boss! It's YOU! And YOU want YOU to work WHEN? Weekends? Nights? Holidays? Even seven days a week if needed? This boss is relentless, and you cannot get away from him/her! He/she is with you every minute of every day 24/7. The worst thing is, if you do not do the tasks your boss says you must do, even if you "go to the office" 50 or 60 hours a week, your boss (now you) will NOT sign a check for you to deposit in your bank like your prior bosses did.

If you don't take care of business every hour of every day, the "freedom" you thought you would receive from a real estate career somehow vanishes. Worry sets in, and fear takes over. That old boss you used to have may now begin to seem pretty good!

So the choice is this: you stay with your current boss (you) and do what it takes. Keep a flexible, yet disciplined schedule and receive a good decent (even terrific) income, *or* you go back to the inflexible schedule and a lesser income and less fulfillment with that other boss.

It is that 3rd level of competence (being "consciously competent") you have to reach in order to succeed in real estate. It gives you the structure you must have. Then you must stay dedicated to the checklists and the tasks.

The truth is, once you master time management, learn the necessary skills, and habits, and have the necessary discipline, you become your own *best boss*, and you become *successful*, with more freedom and enjoyment and the money you were seeking when you started!

> *Discipline Is Just Choosing Between*
> *What You Want Now*
> *And*
> *What You Want Most.*

Freedom?

> *Success Isn't Something That Just Happens —Success Is Learned,*
> *Success Is Practiced*
> *And Then It Is Achieved*

Chapter Five

EFFECTIVE TIME MANAGEMENT

Effective Time Management

> *No Matter How You Feel,*
> *Get Up, Dress Up,*
> *Show Up, And*
> *Never Give Up*

Effective time management: who is control? It is basically a list of all things you must do each day: prioritizing those things, assigning reasonable blocks of time for each of those activities and then following your plan.

The concept is to include on your calendar everything you consider necessary: family activities, anything you feel you should do spiritually, activities for your health and education and, of course, *real estate*. It is important to make sure you have at least 35 to 40 hours per week of focused real estate work booked on your calendar. Most successful real estate agents get their prospecting done every day during a couple of hours or so. I have seen 9:00 a.m. to 11:00 a.m. or 10:00 a.m. to noon for calling or door knocking. I have also seen 4:00 p.m. to 6:00 p.m. or 6:00 p.m. to 8:00 p.m. in the evenings work for prospecting. It doesn't matter when you do it; you simply must DO it!

By checking your emails and voice messages twice per day instead of constantly you can concentrate on your tasks more effectively and accomplish more. I also make sure the phone numbers of my clients and important contacts are in my phone address book so that I can screen the calls to take only the important ones at any given time.

Time management is also all about constantly adding to and adapting your calendar in order to meet changing priorities. If you are married and/or have children, it is extremely important to include your spouse and kids on your calendar. They are probably the reason you need to work in the first place. So you want to make sure they don't *only* get what is left of

Effective Time Management

your time. You must make it a point to put important activities with them on your calendar as a high priority. You certainly do not want to miss the school play, the soccer game your kids have been waiting for, or their choir or solo in the school program!

As for your spouse, I recommend a date night at least one night every week for sure. It is the easiest time to slack off but the most important for you, and your spouse's, well-being. Remember the old saying, "If mama ain't happy, ain't nobody happy!" Well, if "daddy ain't happy," the same goes!

Let's face it. If you neglect your kids or your spouse, undoubtedly there will be a huge price to pay. Furthermore you can't truly be happy or effective at work if you are not happy at home. Therefore, you must put family before your work. Family *must* come first and real estate a close second.

As for your clients, they want your attention as well. But there are proper ways to do that. If you have good time management skills, you can schedule your clients at a *mutually agreeable time. Do NOT allow clients to dictate your schedule.* Many agents think they have to agree to exactly the time the client says, every time. Wait a minute. Don't you normally take the appointment given to you by your dentist or doctor? That is a time you both have available, right? Well, you are the dentist or doctor in this case. Put clients on your schedule at a time that agrees with your schedule, rather than the time *they* want.

You must be in charge of your own calendar and the times you meet. Do NOT allow clients to control your life.

Early in my career I repeated this mistake over and over again. Once I even allowed a lady who called me on a Thanksgiving morning talk me into showing and selling her a home that day. She said it was the only day she could choose, and she was flying in just to pick that house. It ruined Thanksgiving for me and my family. She cancelled two weeks later. For me it meant no gain, a lot of pain and definitely some regret! That day I finally "got it." Just that idea that *you* can be in control of your time will make a huge difference in your life and in your success.

Days off and vacation times off must be included on your calendar to regenerate from the rigors of sales. You should plan at least two days off weekly. Some agents I know take Wednesday or Thursday off plus Sunday. Two weeks of vacation one week at a time should be your minimum. I took off one week per month for several years. Here is a question: what do you do at work just before leaving for vacation? If you are like the rest of us you seriously look at what needs finished or accomplished prior to going so when you get home you are not overwhelmed. It is that extra push (and vacation as a reward!) that makes it possible.

I discovered by continuing to keep in touch with my clients and office by e-mail or text twice daily while on vacation I could have the peace of mind to be free more often. Your smart phone and tablet are your major keys to such freedom. I

Effective Time Management

look at it this way it may take a little time to respond to my clients' needs while I am poolside in Las Vegas but that time is what I need to make the vacation happen in the first place.

Of course if you have a really well trained person who can think like you to cover for you while you are gone then you can cut that cord a bit. However if you truly do care about your clients you will still need to be available for the emergencies while away. It never bothers me and if you can share this with your spouse and kids they will understand. One or two times a day to return calls and problem solve just as normal.

Until I did this it cost me lost sales and commissions when I took that vacation. Now it is a win-win for me. Nothing lost and fun with family and friends gained. It worked on each trip we have taken including cruises and tours around the world. It is a *fun* life!

Chapter Six

PROSPECTING AND MARKETING YOURSELF

Prospecting And Marketing Yourself

> *"Excellence Is Never An Accident;*
> *It Is The Result Of High Intention,*
> *Intelligent Direction, Skillful*
> *Execution and the Vision to See*
> *Obstacles As Opportunities."*
>
> *Anonymous*

Finding buyers and sellers to help. This is sales 101. Every business needs customers to serve. In real estate it is no different. The simple truth is, almost all real estate salespeople are independent contractors who are in business for themselves. That means it is up to most individual agents to find their own customers.

Your business plan could include looking for referrals from other agents or working on a team (as, for example, a buyer's agent, listing agent, or relocation agent), while someone else on the team finds the sellers or buyers. In each such case, however, your income per transaction is lowered, often significantly.

In this book I will focus on the *full-time career agent* who wants to be successful as an *individual agent* running his or her own business. The big question is, how do you find buyers and sellers?

Statistics from the NAR show 70% or more of all the business successful agents have each year comes from their "sphere of influence." So the first action plan as an agent must be to make a list of who knows you and who you know. That's your "sphere of influence." This is an initial list of potential referrals and clients for you to market to during the rest of your career. The goal is to continually touch, and steadily increase, the number of persons on that list. And always be sure to seek first the ones you can help *today,* those who are ready to buy or sell *now.* You will be calling, texting, tweeting, emailing, mailing, posting on Facebook, posting on LinkedIn, talking on the phone or in person with all of these people asking for referrals, and looking for people ready, willing, and able to buy or sell in the immediate future.

Your primary focus is to be *the first agent* they think of calling when they or their friends need EXPERT real estate advice or help. This takes time and frequent reminders of your expertise since at least some of your friends and acquaintances may continue to identify you with your former job or as a friend disassociated from any job whatsoever.

The biggest challenge is that most of the people on your list likely already know *several* dependable agents. Your mission is to continually add more and more potential clients to your list and to get them ALL to see YOU as an unparalled EXPERT in real estate, especially one who lists and sells on a regular basis!

Prospecting is the term used for finding more of these potential clients, and there are multiple ways to prospect. But leads must continually be added to your "sphere of influence" and methodically and routinely contacted thereafter. ("Dripped on. They call it drip marketing.") A short list of ways to find leads includes mega open houses, geographical farming, social farming, group farming, advertising, direct mailing, internet marketing and targeted phone calling.

Colorful and catchy informative newsletters, post cards, notes, thank you cards, social media, digital media, print ads, press releases, signs and everything else you can think of are all ways of prospecting and almost certainly should be a part of your business/marketing plan.

Those agents who lack passion and commitment are the first to fail here because they may be afraid to proclaim the fact that they are selling real estate to their friends and relatives for fear they may not succeed. That being said, typically those agents who focus first on their "sphere of influence" will have more success with less effort. It is easier to remind someone who knows about your ability, and help them, than it is to find new people to help.

Of course you must always be seeking to build your clientele by listening for the signs of people who may be about to move. Your antenna must be up at all times. One of the ways to constantly be aware of people you may be able to help is to learn to routinely ask questions of all those you meet or communicate with questions that ultimately lead to finding out their situation and that lead them to learn you are in real estate and can help them or other people they know. Asking and listening to full, deep answers are major keys to success. When the opportunity presents itself, you should ask more and more detailed questions in order to get to the real motivations of prospects. You will want to ask for details in order to learn if you are to be able to help them or their friends, now or in the future.

Once you have met someone, it's always a good idea to ask them what *they* do for a living (which invariably requires that they learn what *you* do). You can say, "I am looking for buyers and sellers I can help, especially now with such low rates and home prices. Do you happen to know anyone who is thinking of buying or selling in the coming weeks or months or even in the next year or so?" A lot of people (and maybe your new friend) have put off moving, making them real potential clients. If they say they are thinking of moving, you have more questions to ask in order to qualify them further.

Remember this: you should never put a buyer in your car without qualifying him or her first. Thus, you must be certain to *listen,* very carefully, to each and every answer a prospective client provides. While many people may not know it, true listening is a skill all to itself, and its importance cannot be over-stated. You might think, "Well, everybody with hearing 'listens'," but there is a vast difference between "hearing" what someone says versus being an "active listener" and not only hearing but mentally absorbing every phrase and nuance of what is said to you.

Marketing yourself. It is said you can build your business with "sweat equity" *or* "check equity" (calling or visiting lots of people) *or* spending money to buy leads and receiving calls from money spent on advertising and promotions. Either way works. In both cases, you ultimately have to speak on the phone or in person to make the sale. Advertising also eats away at your net income of course; so if you choose to advertise, you must closely watch the return on your invested dollars. Too often agents spend so much on advertising and promotions that there is little money left to live on even from a number of sales.

"When You Want To Be the Best ....Only an Expert Will Do!"

Either way you choose, "sweat equity" or check equity, as your system of marketing, you will have basic marketing expenses such as brochures, business cards, flyers, newsletters and website costs. Your brochure will include your unique selling proposition, your mission statement and something that focuses on your clients' needs as well as how you can serve them. Your marketing plan should reinforce your image as an EXPERT REALTOR®. The flyers and newsletters you use must be informative and show YOU as their compelling choice for EXPERT real estate service. Of course, you should have a presence through a website, social media and e-mails as well.

Buying leads or "check equity" gives you the possible advantage of having leads come to you without knocking on doors or cold calling. The challenge is to find the right medium (internet, direct mail, newspaper, magazine advertising, etc.) at a reasonably low cost to make it profitable and productive. Invariably the lead-generating system you use will require calling many leads back and trying to connect via their voicemail or e-mail with uncertain results.

The most successful and profitable system of marketing yourself usually combines a little of both "sweat equity" and "check equity." It begins by building your list of potential clients (again, as your "sphere of influence") from people you already know and who you are in contact with: friends, family, social groups and possibly people from sports and religious activities. Your goal is to add to that list and market to them regularly, seeking referrals and new business. Your contacts with them should always reinforce your image as an EXPERT in real estate and the one they should call when they or their friends need the services you offer.

No matter how you choose to go about it, you must proactively search each day for people to help. In the final analysis there are only two ways to do that: eyeball to eyeball or ear to ear. And you always need to know what to say, how to say it, and when to say it when you do make contact.

> *Be Brave Enough To Start A Conversation That Matters.*

Chapter Seven

QUALIFYING ALL THE TIME

Qualifying All The Time

> *"You Get In Life What You Have The Courage To Ask For."*
>
> *-Oprah Winfrey*

Qualifying Prospects–Asking lots of questions and listening. There are six basic qualifying questions you must always ask in sales of any kind. They help you determine if you have a qualified person to help before you spend much time or effort with them. In real estate you ask these questions even before the first appointment, usually when initially talking with just one of the decision makers. You will ask these same questions once again, in more depth, at your first appointment when all decision makers *must* be present. The answers may be different for each decision maker. This will be your chance to do some basic, but extremely important, questioning to bring all decision makers to agreement on what they want and who they want to represent them.

The six questions for you to ask initially and in your first appointment with all decision-makers are:

1) *"Are you committed to another REALTOR®, brand, course of action, or sales person?"*

2) *"Who are the decision makers? You and your spouse? Or do you have a third party who influences your decision or lends money, etc.?"*

3) *"What are you looking for as far as location, size, price, amenities, etc.?"*

4) *"How do you plan to pay for it? How much cash down and at closing? And what amount of mortgage and payment do you anticipate? Have you been qualified by a lender?"*

Qualifying All The Time

5) "Why are you wanting to move?" (This is the motivation question.) You should also ask on a scale of one to ten (ten being the highest) what is your motivation to move?

6) "When would you like to be able to move? Is there a specific deadline to be moved? If so, by what month and date?"

Setting appointments. If you have received appropriate answers from the prospect at the start, and it looks like you could help him or her, you can say: "It sounds like I may be able to help you, but I don't know. The only way we will know for sure is to meet with you and your spouse (and any other decision makers) to find out. At that time I promise it will be worth your time, no matter if we work together or not. I will help save you a lot of time by getting you way ahead in the process of buying or selling your home, no matter who you decide to use as your agent."

"There will be three possible outcomes to our appointment. First, we will discover if I can help you, and we all agree to work together to buy or sell your home, which would be nice because I want to help you if I can. Second, you decide that for some reason we cannot work together. Or third, I decide I cannot help you, or I cannot work with you. Any of the three outcomes is possible."

"What times are usually best for both you and your spouse? Evenings or weekends?" *Always make that appointment even if it is a tentative appointment to be confirmed!* And never proceed without meeting *all* decision makers at your first appointment for sure. From my experience, real disappointment

"When You Want To Be the Best ….Only an Expert Will Do!"

and hurt almost always follows if you break this rule. Remember my two experiences when this happened?

Remember, more than one decision maker means two or more distinct personalities, wants and desires. It also means there might be other real estate people they know or to whom they may be committed. In the event they cancel and do not re-schedule, and if you cannot meet with both of them, let them go. And keep looking for others you can help with the time you might spend.

You may have to do some preliminary ground work speaking with your initial contact. The purpose would be to gain enough information prior to meeting with all decision makers so that you are properly prepared for your presentation. For example, you may want to visit the seller's property prior to your presentation in order to know the characteristics of the home as compared to those already on the market. The idea is to get a feel for the right price of the home.

My scars are there from the times I spent hours and days and a tremendous amount of gasoline showing homes to one person without being paid. Even though those scars have healed, I did not forget those situations, nor will you, if you EVER allow them to happen to you.

You can see that by following the above, you are not promising the moon and neither are you taking them right out to see properties. Rather, you are acting like a professional REALTOR®.

Qualifying All The Time

Gaining trust. The beauty is when you ask the appropriate questions it leads your clients to believe you really know what you are doing. When you meet for the appointment, you will use a buyer or seller workbook or presentation book to further guide the process. Qualifying is nothing more than asking questions and listening. People trust those who they feel really care by listening and those who know what to do in a logical sequence. It is said **"People do not care how much you know until they know how much you care about them."**

You must always have systems in place and follow those systems to best serve your clients. They will see your actions and respond accordingly.

So let's review. Confirm the appointment ahead of time. Make sure all of the decision makers attend. If there is more than one decision maker, and only one person shows up, re-schedule. As you know from my experience it is important to do this even if the one who shows up insists they have agreed that whatever home that person finds will be the one they buy. They will say the second person will only confirm the choice. Let them go if they do not re-schedule. Better still; sell them on the importance of all parties being on the same page.

If they confirm and show up, that's great. If they do not show up or keep putting you off without re-scheduling, then obviously they are not going to work with you. It isn't that important to them or the spouse has a different plan. Your time is valuable. Just move on to a serious buyer or seller.

I repeat; do not waste time with people who do not meet for your appointment. Remember, the purpose of the presentation at the appointment is to qualify them and get a written commitment to work together on your terms. Your terms will be defined in detail during that appointment and cannot be relayed to another.

Point blank, you *must connect* with, and *ask questions* of, *all* participants before you know if you can help them or decide to commit your time to help them; qualify them.

Be Picky With Who You Invest Your Time In.
Wasted Time Is Worse Than Wasted Money

Qualifying All The Time

> *"The Most Common Way People Give Up Their Power Is By Thinking They Don't Have Any."*
>
> *-Alice Walker*

Chapter Eight

PRESENTING

Presenting

> *Your Life Is Your Message To The World.*
> *Make Sure It's Inspiring.*

Presenting. At the appointment with buyers or sellers (all decision makers), your presentation should include a workbook or checklist, which includes all of those qualifying questions as discussed in the previous chapter in a more detailed written form. (Are you committed to another agent? Who? What? How? Why? and When?) At the end of the appointment, you will have a final *written agreement to work together* or an agreement not to work together. Of course, if you prefer not to work with them, you can refer them to another agent who you feel might be better suited to them and possibly obtain a referral fee from that agent if and when they do sell or buy.

One of the most important decisions you will make is *whether you* will work with *them* or not. You MUST plan to work *only* with ready, willing and able buyers and sellers who are teachable about the market and have a high motivation.

Showing what you can do. Included in your presentation for buyers or sellers is your "Unique Selling Proposition," the simpler the better. It can be as simple as a Mission Statement, which provides the reasons anyone should use *your* services rather than another agent's. It answers the question: "What do you do that is different and unique in the eyes of your potential client?" It is based on who you are, your particular abilities, and your knowledge of the market as well as your knowledge of the real estate values and locations in the communities and areas you serve. You must know and have confidence that you can perform according to your own "Unique Selling Proposition." For a seller you prepare a pre-listing package with your emphasis being on them and

Presenting

demonstrating to them your uniqueness. Your presentation becomes a confirmation of it and the affirmation, in writing, that you are their absolute best choice. Your total commitment to their best interest can be seen through your mission statement, checklists, procedures and questions you ask and LISTEN to. It MUST be a part of your uniqueness and why they should choose YOU! It is a fact many people do not think highly of sales people, and as a real estate sales person who shows you personally have their best interest at heart, you are unique.

When someone agrees to work with you, they are trusting you to help them with one of their most important financial and personal decisions. It is a lot like trusting the dentist or doctor. These professionals have a thorough pre-exam questionnaire and checklist. Can you imagine visiting a doctor for the first time who asks you, "What's wrong?" You say "headache," and he gives you medicine or a pain reliever without a questionnaire or series of detailed health questions. He would not know if you are allergic to certain medications or have other conditions or issues. Would you feel you could trust him?

The more thorough you are, the higher the level of trust. You focus on finding out exactly who your clients are, what they are looking for, and what they want as an end result. *It is all about them*, with your intent being to give them what they want.

Getting their commitment. In your presentations (to both buyers and sellers), you must always have a memorized and well-rehearsed dialogue made up of a series of questions, the answers to which lead to a mutual commitment to work together. And you get that commitment in writing.

I am repeating on purpose because this is important. Just like a doctor or a dentist, you too are a professional, and you should never start operating until you have fully assessed your client's needs. Do not give away your time and service until you have a firm commitment that they will work *exclusively* with you. If you break this rule, your value is diminished in their eyes because you are acting like all other real estate agents. So *you* must be different. *You* are a professional who knows what to do, when to do it, and how to do it. *You are an "EXPERT."*

The validity of this system has proven itself many times over when my new committed clients pulled out a listing they received from another agent and said, "Please show us this home." Obviously, the other agent was never paid for his or her time or effort.

Presenting

> *The Expert In Anything*
> *Was Once a Beginner.*

"When You Want To Be the Best ….Only an Expert Will Do!"

Chapter Nine

MENTORING YOUR CLIENTS

Mentoring Your Clients

> "The Best Way To Predict The Future
> Is To
> Create It."
>
> -Peter Drucker

Selling is mentoring your clients by discovering what they want and educating, reminding, and guiding clients to make, or re-make, a choice to act to accomplish what they want. You can see why some of the most successful agents are trained or natural teachers and educators.

Helping clients make informed decisions. Now, the answers to the qualifying questions you asked of the buyers or sellers through your intense listening skills become the basis of your actions. You know what they want. Now your focus is on helping them accomplish their specific goals.

Many people are uninformed about the process of buying and selling real estate. They may expect agents to advise them what to do. If your clients have that expectation, it is your job to correct and inform them of their responsibilities in any sale. All decisions must be theirs. You present facts and information for their use in coming to good conclusions.

In selling or buying, you are the one who must make sure they know the market well enough to make informed decisions. They need to make good choices about price and terms based on location and outside influences such as market demand, interest rates, direction of the market, and competition. You must keep them realistic and on track through the entire process, always staying focused on their motivation and time frames.

Finding their new home. The system is easy but thorough. It starts with the first premise which is that we can only choose from homes that are currently on the market. Remember, you ONLY work with people who are ready, willing and able to buy NOW. Therefore, it is a matter of choosing which home is the best for them from those available at that time.

The second premise is there is likely NO "perfect" home that meets ALL of their price, location, and other needs and desires. They MUST be at least somewhat willing to compromise and adjust in order to buy a home at all. The best example is my own situation when on one occasion my wife and I set out to buy. We wanted a bigger home and much preferred Rancho Bernardo since we had lived there for years. That bigger home we wanted did not exist in the price range and location we desired. However, by buying in the neighboring town in South Escondido, we saved at least $100,000 and obtained a better home with a four car garage (an unexpected, but fantastic plus!), and it was only minutes away from our friends in Rancho Bernardo.

The third premise is that your clients must know to choose or reject each home on the basis of its particular merits, which can only be seen in person. Pictures and videos never tell the whole story. You must make sure your clients understand this. It is your job to teach them and *show them*.

However, every time before taking them out to show them homes, you should meet with them (preferably at your office) to review and choose which homes to see and in what order you will see them. You prepare a detailed list of the homes on the market that meet their needs, based on only three preliminary criteria: 1) location (zip codes) and neighborhoods; 2) year built (indicates home styles, amenities and potential condition); and 3) square footage (size of the home your clients desire). The list should also include a "Competitive" Market Analysis also sometimes called "Comparative" Marketing Analysis (CMA), showing not only available homes, but also those pending sales, *and* those sold in recent months in the areas they have chosen. The CMA listings will also show location, number of bedrooms, number of bathrooms, garage size, size of lot, and more. Your clients will eliminate some from the list of available homes, based on *their choice* at that time, never yours.

Now proceed to narrow the search. Remember my own situation? My wife and I found our home by looking in the neighboring community to meet our needs. Always be mindful of the options they have if they find it hard to find a home where they initially preferred to live. Many times I have found the home for my clients in an entirely different area away from their original preference. It was a result of my knowledge of the surrounding communities and my ability to ask the right questions when I first met them.

By showing them all the homes that meet their criteria (including those in the CMA), they will gain the ability to price the home they pick with accurate knowledge of the current market. Of course, you are teaching and updating them as you go along, and as you show them homes, you give them the assignment of choosing their top three homes (first, second and third) as you go through the process of seeing each home.

Mentoring Your Clients

Once you have narrowed the homes to the three they are willing to buy, zero in on the one they want first and write the offer. If they cannot come to terms with that seller, you then go to the next. Your job is to give them realistic, accurate information as they make price and terms decisions. It is at this point as they try to get the lowest price possible that many people lose track mentally of their initial motivation. They forget they have chosen this particular home for certain features that made them consider it best. You must resell them on the home by reminding them why they chose it. **Selling is educating, reminding, and guiding clients to make, or re-make, a choice.** Since you have already found two other homes, you can easily help them consider their options and the reasons they picked that one in the first place. It also gets down to how motivated they are to buy a home, and especially that home. Motivation is everything. It is the glue that keeps the process together.

Sometimes even if they have to pay a little more than they really want to, time will increase the value of the home. In the meantime, they are living in the home they really wanted. Keeping your focus on their goal, their motivation, and using your ability to communicate makes it all happen. It is selling them what they want.

Selling their home. When you are working for the sellers, your job is likewise to use all of your available resources to sell the home. **You are being paid to sell.** You should focus on selling the property with the most effective tools you can muster. One of the most important and effective tools (especially when establishing the asking price for any property) is, once again, the CMA. In addition, it is a good idea to take the client to actually *see* the active competitive properties on the CMA. Viewing the properties first hand and utilizing the CMA will allow you to aid the seller in establishing an *appropriate* price. Just as when working with buyers, you will have a checklist of all the things you will do to bring as many buyers and agents to the property you can. And you will do so until the property is sold! Price it right, and it will sell!

Now you just have to use **your selling ability** find and inform the potential buyer of the benefits of owning the home through your media and advertising systems.

You may have noticed I emphasized the term **"sell"**. What I have discovered is most people think that is a nasty word until they realize how you can truly be an honest, trustworthy person who has the best interests of their clients at heart and **sell** real estate. When you think of it that is true of selling most anything useful.

Another key to selling is the use of memorized phrases and questions to assist in communicating with clients. Yet many people who want to be real estate **sales** people object to memorizing those phrases because they do not want to sound like they are making people do what they do not want to do. If you really do memorize exact words to say in the right way you will not sound that way.

Mentoring Your Clients

This is too important so please forgive me for repeating this again. (Repetition is an educational tool.) **Selling is mentoring your clients** by discovering what they want and educating, reminding, and guiding clients to make, or re-make, a choice to act to accomplish what they want.

> *"I Have Been Impressed With The Urgency Of Doing. Knowing Is Not Enough; We Must Apply. Being Willing Is Not Enough; We Must Do*
>
> *-Leonardo Da Vinci*

Chapter Ten

BUILDING A BUSINESS FOR LIFE

Building a Business for Life

> *Sales Go Up And Down..*
>
> *Service Stays Forever*

> *"Motivation Is What Gets You Started.*
> *Habit Is What Keeps You Going."*
>
> *-Jim Rohn*

Your goal should be to build a business for life. In fact, the previous chapters mentioned your sphere of influence as your foundation. So far in this book your focus on asking questions and listening and showing you care has taken you to the point at which you have a signed listing or a signed agreement to purchase through you. Your customer service now continues as you either have a buyer or seller with an offer to sign or accept.

Contract through escrow. I repeat again Whether representing buyers or sellers, you should make sure your clients are the ones making ALL the decisions concerning ALL terms of the sale. In other words, you should NOT allow them to say to you that they "trust you" because you are the professional. Simply because you know the process and details of buying and selling better than they do does not mean you are in any position to make ANY decisions on behalf of the client. What you do instead is to make sure they receive all the information they need in order to make good decisions. This must be true even when helping others from other cultures who insist on trusting you.

By following this rule every time – in every buying and selling situation – you virtually eliminate any liability, including any that may linger after the sale – which could otherwise have unpleasant legal ramifications for you and your clients let alone remove the possibility of helping them in another sale.

Accordingly, you must know how to create buying and selling contracts that are in the best interest of your clients. You must also know how to carry that accepted contract thru Escrow.

It is also extremely important to make sure the contract provides full protection from negative impacts as a result of the purchase or sale. For example, each contract should detail the typical terms and requirements, including not only clear title, insurance, and contingencies, but other terms such as dates of possession and condition of property at date of legal transfer of title. It should also be a legally binding and enforceable contract.

The contract for the buyers should allow them a "contingency period," during which time they are given full disclosures (from the sellers and agents) of everything they may know or observe concerning the condition of the property and particularly any problem or problems that may exist with such things as electrical, plumbing, structural, roof, heating and air conditioning, etc. The buyers must be informed of any title issues, easements, assessments, liens, etc. that may be attached to the property that they will need to know and contend with. Finally, the buyers should also have full access to the property during the contingency period in order to inspect it for themselves in detail, utilizing professionals of their choice in order to determine whether or not the property is a good fit for them before removing their contingencies and continuing to purchase it.

Likewise, if you are representing the sellers, your contract should protect them from possible legal action by the buyers. Sellers must be sure to provide complete disclosures to buyers concerning the property, and the surrounding property, that would or could have an adverse impact upon the continued use of the property or desirability of the property now or in the future.

Once you have an offer to purchase, which contains all the terms, contingencies, etc. signed by both buyers and sellers (i.e. a contract), now what? Because **this is a people business, not just a house-selling or property-selling business**, your job as an agent/REALTOR® is like a pilot of a plane. You have gone through all of your pre-flight checklists and pulled away from the terminal and taken off. A lot could still happen before you arrive at your final destination (i.e. the "close of escrow" and transfer of deed). During this period (the actual flight), you should be aware that something could go wrong that causes the entire process (and all your work and effort) to be aborted.

To illustrate, my wife and I had such an experience on an airplane one time shortly after takeoff from the Dallas airport. It wasn't fun, but fortunately because of the ability and knowledge of our pilot, we had a happy ending. During assent, suddenly one of the plane's engines caught fire. As a result, the pilot continued to accelerate rapidly (in order to put the fire out) and then banked sharply to circle back and land on the same runway going in the opposite direction. As we approached the landing strip, the plane was still nearly at 90 degrees to the runway, until the very last second, when the pilot expertly leveled off for what turned out to be a perfect landing. That pilot is definitely one I would want again! And the airline knew to give us what we wanted and needed at that time. They didn't want that incident to deter us from getting where we wanted to go when we wanted to be there. So they immediately put us all on another plane, and we were all on our way again within an hour.

The real estate process has a similar abortion period as well when buyers have a period of time to inspect and possibly reject the property. We just turn back cancel the contract and continue buying or selling just as our airline did by immediately getting us to our destination on another plane,.

Your job is to stay focused on your clients' need to buy or sell a home. You must follow the contract (flight plan) and make sure all of its terms and conditions are met for a smooth landing (closing). This includes making sure all the papers and documents are passed to each party for approval on time. Just like an airline flight, there are sometimes rough landings and sometimes difficult approaches to landings as you get closer to the close of escrow. Packing and preparing for the move, mover's scheduling and delays, and much more often cause problems beyond our control. We must nevertheless overcome them. All this can be as emotional as flying blind in fog or through rough weather as you approach your destination.

You, as the pilot, must be the calm in the middle of the storm in order to help your clients through this time. *You* must demonstrate *your ability* to get them to where they want to go so they will want to have you as their pilot again and again, *and* they will also want to refer their families and friends to you because you got them safely to their destination.

As I have said this is a people business. What I describe above are the emotions turbulence caused by stress of moving and by things that happen when people feel they have little or no control. The truth is there are a great number of people involved in an escrow. The buyers the sellers the agents on both sides, their transaction coordinators, their brokers, the escrow officer, the escrow assistant, the title officers, the loan officer, the loan processor, the loan underwriter, the funder, the lien holders who must release the liens, the appraisers, the inspectors of all kinds, the notary and curriers all have to perform their duties and on time to close the escrow when your clients want it closed so their movers can move on schedule. We also have the property the buyers are selling must go through the same process in order for them to have the money to buy.

Repeat customers and referrals. Now once the transfer of title to the property occurs, the old saying goes; "If the buyers aren't happy, ain't nobody happy" (except the attorneys). So just like the pilot of that aircraft, it is up to you, the EXPERT real estate sales agent/REALTOR®, to make sure the buyers know exactly, in writing, what they are purchasing and that their expectations are being met. By drawing up the contract and making sure it is properly followed, your clients will see and appreciate your attentiveness to their best interest. They will be more likely to ask for your help in the future when they are ready to buy again *and* to refer you to their friends and family as well.

Building a Business for Life

In all of this process of buying-selling and during the "escrow period" (the time between an accepted offer and closing), buyers and sellers are typically stressed much like those airline passengers. It is often not easy for anyone involved. My experience is there are sometimes as many as six to eight personalities directly involved in the transaction, and their emotions can easily upset a sale. Your job is to manage the emotions of all of them (including your own), keeping all heads cool and calm. As I mentioned before, you may have two buyers, two sellers, two agents and possibly two spouses of agents, who contribute to the emotional level of the transaction.

Looking closely at the buyer and the seller couples, one of the spouses wants or needs to make the move of their household and the other may NOT want to make the move because they are attached to neighbors, friends, schools, church, the location where they live, etc. It is because of necessity they must move. Say it is the wife and mother who loves the home she has made, but the husband lost his job or is transferred. You, the REALTOR®, list the home and find a buyer. Mrs. Buyer comes in and says she will need to redecorate Mrs. Seller's home that was recently updated to Mrs. Seller's taste. Mrs. Seller feels her home is going to be ruined by this new buyer. She takes it personally, through no fault of the buyer, and she does not want Mrs. Buyer to come to her home again until it is hers. Her first emotion is she just does not want to sell to that person. Guess what? Mrs. Buyer may have the same feelings about leaving her home!

These are real-world, real-life experiences. It is best to know this in advance and make sure the sellers and buyers have virtually no contact from the start. That is why we ask sellers to leave their home when it is being shown and not be present throughout the inspection process unless supervised by agents.

It is absolutely imperative that buyers and sellers do not meet without both agents present and under the right terms and conditions. The only time I recommend permitting buyers and sellers to meet is at the property during the property inspection, with strict rules to limit all questions to the property itself and NEVER discuss terms or conditions of the sale, let alone what the buyer will do with decorations! Agents are the conduit and catalyst for all negotiations to be successful.

So this is the essence of building a great career: superior service, knowledge and commitment that leads to repeat business and referral business.

Building a business for life. Your job is also to ASK for those referrals. From time to time after your successful flight with each client, you will want to remind them that you are still in the real estate business and ready to serve them and their friends whenever they need you or need real estate information. That's right! They must be nurtured in your "past clients and sphere of influence list" (Chapter 5). And the beat goes on…

Building a Business for Life

> *"Always Do Your best. What You Plant Now,
> You Will Harvest Later."*
>
> *-Og Mandino*

> *"Quality Questions Create A Quality Life. Successful People Ask Better Questions, And As A Result, They Get Better Answers."*
>
> *-Anthony Robbins*

Chapter Eleven

TECHNOLOGY AND REAL ESTATE SALES

Technology and Real Estate Sales

> *You Must Have The Most Up To Date Tools Of The Trade To Compete In The 21st Century*

Technology and real estate sales. You must have the most up to date tools for your real estate career. They are important for communicating with your clientele, for accessing the listings, tools and information you need to service your clients. Here is a basic list of the tools you should have:

Internet access.

A smart phone. For texting, email, internet and document access.

A newer laptop or desktop. Your laptop must have wifi access and must have an office suite compatible with Microsoft Office and with a good browser installed so you can access your.online REALTOR® Association's websites for their tools and information as well as key real estate marketing sites and services you choose.

A tablet. It can be an Ipad or Android and must be wifi enabled.

Good phone service for your area.

Dependable e-mail service. I prefer Google's gmail.

Your mls access.

Your Facebook and Linkedin pages with profiles established and on your devices. Others like Twitter Circles and Pinterest to reach a wider audience.

You will go online to access important online services to help market you and your listings. They allow you to create and

Technology and Real Estate Sales

send out cards, flyers, and mailings of all kind online. You don't even have to touch them or take them to the post office. However, if your budget demands it, you can still find less expensive printing services and you can still save by doing the mailings yourself. It is a matter of time and budget.

You need a good customer relations management system. (CRM) This will allow you to calendar and follow up automatically by email, keep track of your communications, and remind you of tasks you need to perform to prospect, manage your sales and maintain your sphere of influence contacts. The right program will be like an assistant and will keep you busy doing the pre-programmed tasks you decided upon. It will help keep you on track. Today many people use "Top Producer" or Microsoft Outlook but there are many to choose from. Including Google products.

Your contracts will be online and your documents will be online. We in California use the zipforms provided by our state association for our contracts. Google has a business suite that includes online document storage with good features such as gmail, websites you can design yourself, social media, an online document storage and many more features

You will need an easy to use remote document signature program. Today Docusign is the most popular. Our state association has a free signature program as well.

You will constantly need to monitor the latest technology tools as they evolve in order to keep up in our fast moving, innovative economy.

"When You Want To Be the Best ....Only an Expert Will Do!"

Chapter Twelve

THOUGHTS, TIPS AND MYTHS

Thoughts, Tips and Myths

> *Before You Act, Listen.*
> *Before You React, Think.*
> *Before You Spend, Earn.*
> *Before You Criticize, wait.*
> *Before You Pray, Forgive.*
> *Before You Quit, Try.*

"When You Want To Be the Best ….Only an Expert Will Do!"

Some real estate sales thoughts, tips and myths:

Advertising in glossy magazines: For some reason, sellers think these things sell homes. Granted, sometimes a home may be seen for the first time in one of these, but the reality is it is a lavish expense that mainly gives the seller the feeling the listing agent is doing a great job. It feeds the ego of the seller and the ego of the agent. I gave in to the demands of one of my sellers when I was younger and put an ad in one of these popular magazines. Thousands of dollars and not one call.

Most agents will never need this type of advertising with the exception of the multi- million dollar homes and very exclusive international jet-set home magazines.

Full page display advertising in newspapers: Same thing. I have worked in offices where these types of ads are common place with the phone numbers in the ads coming into the real estate company where the phone is answered by an agent other than the one who listed the property. Sellers love the ads, but reality is they mainly interest sellers who think it would be great. And have you ever called on those ads? When you do, you will get a newly licensed person who will often not know anything about the property. These people fumble the call and the sellers lose a potential buyer.

You should always get the calls on all ads when you list properties to sell. You are the most motivated and knowledgeable person concerning that property.

Thoughts, Tips and Myths

Real estate agent caravans: This one is deceiving for new agents until they realize they can be one of the biggest time wasters ever devised by man. Agents have come up with the idea they need to promote their listings to other agents. Yet this is an ancient ritual from real estate sales from before we had paper listing books. Since we are in the 21st century, it makes no sense to have agents go to a social hour with coffee and donuts and fruit to pitch pictures and minimal information to other agents when all the information (and much, much more) is instantaneously available when it is uploaded to the MLS, Multiple Listing Service, and Internet when they get the listing. The fact is many of the agents who regularly go are more interested in socializing and eating than selling real estate. It makes them feel like they are doing something in their career.

Sellers, too, think it is great to have all these people going through their home. Of course they think they will be the ones who will sell it. Not likely! The one who sells it will be the disciplined agent who has a buyer and shows all the homes that qualify in their price range and location. That agent never needs coaxing to see the home she or he sells. They just look on the MLS when they have a buyer.

Of course you will see the great listing agents at those caravans. They only do it because their sellers expect it and sometimes just because of their ego. Unfortunately if my seller insists, I might be talked into it, but I will tell them the truth first. Of course if you like the social side, and you feel ok with spending the time, I guess you can join the party.

I decided to pass on the caravans when I looked at my priorities. My choice was between going to early morning caravans or seeing my kids more by taking them to school. I know I made the right choice. I enjoyed my kids and got to know them better.

Mentoring: I was in my early 30's when I started in real estate. I was given a desk between two "experienced" ladies who had been in the business several years. They both took an interest in me to teach me the business. One decided she would mentor me in how to do an open house and find buyers. She set up the stakes etc. drawing people in. The home we were showing was a three bedroom near a busy street so we did have people interested in seeing it from those open house signs. She got busy talking to some people who came in, and this nice couple came in so I engaged in conversation with them by myself and asked them what they were looking for. They said they owned a four bedroom home and wanted to downsize to a smaller home preferably a two bedroom. I asked them if this was a home they would consider. They said "no." It was still just a bit too large. The lady just did not want a lot of house to take care of. About that time my "mentor" came over full of enthusiasm and interrupted and asked them if they thought this was the right home for them. They said "no." She immediately, enthusiastically, told them she had the "perfect" home for them just two streets up and energetically got them to follow her to go see that home. That home was a four bedroom home... Enough said?

Thoughts, Tips and Myths

I had the habit from my prior sales experience and training of really focusing on what people I talked to wanted and whether they were qualified, motivated and able to buy. So when I sold my first home, the other "mentor" asked me what I had sold, where, and the price. When I told her, she quickly responded, "I never would have allowed one of my clients to pay that much for that home." I found out, 35 years later, my client still owned that home, and it was worth eight times what she paid for it with her FHA low down payment. My "mentor" was the one who proudly showed me a list of her clients who said they wanted to buy. I don't remember her selling anyone in the next three or four months. I could not understand why she would not sell them homes while I was finding people and helped them one at a time and never really had a list with more than three or four I was actively showing and selling to. She was another "experienced" mentor.

Some real estate companies match new agents with experienced agents who are somewhat successful. The trouble is those agents have their own clients who naturally take priority over the needs of a new agent. And most offices hand a new agent over to an active selling agent who will get a cut of the new agent's commission as an incentive. Too often that mentor focuses on getting a sale accomplished and often has little time or inclination to really teach the new agent except to say, "Watch what I do." I have been told that by many agents I have interviewed from other companies.

How do you best learn? By watching or doing?

"When You Want To Be the Best ….Only an Expert Will Do!"

What I do and recommend is your mentor teaches you how to do it yourself so you can learn by doing. When you have a question or issue, he or she should be available to answer your questions all along the way. It has to do with preparation and execution with someone backing you up by phone and one on one sessions.

Seminars: I highly recommend seminars by top sales trainers who specialize in real estate. They always have very good systems and procedures that are very useful. That said, it is important to know how they make money. They are not selling real estate. They are selling training and coaching, especially coaching that brings in a lot of repeat money from a lot of motivated agents. As much as $1,500 per month or more per month. Coaching is an art form, and it takes a special person to coach. Most seminar speakers have a large number of coaches, some good, some not so good. I was totally surprised when a newer broker I met told me he was a coach. I knew he only had a few years in the business and yet he was coaching.

If you are lucky, you will find one who connects with you and who will bring out your best. The problem is it is all up to you whether you will do what it takes to succeed. I have been coached and have been coaching agents myself for years. It is all up to you. If you know what to do, all a coach can do is remind you of what you must do and hold you accountable. If you are a person who needs that person by your side to root for you and reflect your goals and action plan back to you, then you may be prime for a good coach and that will surely be worth way more than $1,500 per month.

Thoughts, Tips and Myths

It would be an advantage to choose a company to work for whose broker or trainer also coaches and holds you accountable. Depending on how you learn sometimes paying a good amount of money for coaching gives you that extra incentive to keep on task so you do not waste that money. I know that did seem to be something I thought of when I was being coached. When I knew my call was coming tomorrow I was more likely to be ready.

As for me as a coach, I focus on systems and habits and start from the beginning one thing at a time-one step at a time to build a strong foundation for your business. That would be starting with your "sphere of influence." From that group you should always have over 70% of your business every year. You decide your priorities from session to session. I hold you accountable by asking your progress and reviewing business plan and your challenges with it. Everything else is based on the principles in this book. One system at a time. You learning and doing the work.

While you are selling and building your career in residential real estate you should take every opportunity to learn everything you can about our tax laws and especially the IRS code section 1031. That code allows you to exchange property held for investment selling and buying the next property of higher value all the while deferring taxes indefinitely. It is fun. You can learn these strategies by taking the Commercial Investment courses provided by the National Association of REALTORS® affiliate. Given as a part of courses required to become a Certified Commercial Investment Member, CCIM.

Chapter Thirteen

BEYOND RESIDENTIAL REAL ESTATE

> "Nothing Will Work Unless You Do."
>
> -Maya Angelou

You may find your passion beyond residential Real Estate. One of the wonderful characteristics of Real Estate as a career is once you have your license you can decide to go into many other facets of the business and find your niche for your career. That can include *mortgage brokering* (residential or commercial), *residential income brokerage* (including wealth building using IRS section 1031 tax deferred exchange opportunities to accumulate net worth and income), *commercial sales and leasing* (retail, office, or industrial properties), land sales (lots to acres including agricultural properties), *land development* and re-development, *syndications* for real estate investing, *appraising*, selling *business opportunities*, or even *timeshare sales* or vacation rentals, and *property management* of all types of real estate.

The important thing to remember is the *basic principles* in the sale of residential real estate continue to apply in the other aspects of the business. *In each* you will have to find (*prospect* for) clients, *qualify* clients (are they committed to another agent or broker, find out who the decision makers are, what they want to accomplish, how will they pay for it, why they want to do it (the motivation at what level-on a scale of one to ten), and when do they want to do it. You'll also *present* to clients, to ALL decision makers, using a series of questions, the answers to which lead to a *mutual commitment* to work together. And you must be able to *deliver* on your commitment in an EXPERT way so as to establish a high level of *trust for future business and referrals.*

Beyond Residential Real Estate

Each of these real estate career paths requires specialized knowledge, commitment and experience to be successful. Ultimately you may find your passion in one of these areas rather than in residential real estate sales. I gravitated early to investment real estate but found many people who own investments own their own home or multiple residential homes, condos, or apartments. Indeed, it has been fun to be able to sell homes and also help my friends and clients build their net worth through the 1031 system of exchanging up. That is the way both my wife Paula and I have gained equity so that in our senior years we have a good income. Review the last paragraph of the preceding chapter. You will find your educational and career options well categorized by going onto the National Association of REALTORS® website, Nar.org.

But again, you are at level 2 (consciously incompetent). It is all up to you. You have a lifetime of learning ahead of you to build your career. I wish you the best.

Onward! Upward!!

Chapter Fourteen

REVIEW OF WHAT YOU LEARNED

Review of What You Learned

*There Is No Elevator To Success.
You Have To Take The Stairs.*

Review, did you:

Find out the major hurdles and obstacles to a successful real estate career?

Discover the means and methods of helping others buy and sell real estate?

Get a glimpse into the emotions of agents, buyers and sellers?

Find the keys to balanced, satisfying and rewarding real estate career?

Learn what to do to get your license and stay in the business for life?

Learn the major mistakes most agents make and how to avoid them?

Remember... Be Only an EXPERT!

Review of What You Learned

What did you learn about:

Your passion?	Commitment?
Your attitude?	Who is your boss?
Your freedom?	Who is in control?
Your self discipline?	Vacations?
Time Management?	Marketing?
Prospecting?	Selling?
Qualifying?	Presenting?
Mentoring?	Tips and Myths?
Technology?	Beyond Real Estate?

Building Your Busines for Life?

Where to go for information?

Is Real Estate Sales Right For Your? (check the next chapter for more thoughts)

Joe can be reached in San Diego, California by calling or texting (858) 967-8801. He will be glad to meet with you to help you further decide on this career opportunity.

Chapter Fifteen

IS REAL ESTATE SALES RIGHT FOR YOU?

Is Real Estate Sales Right For You?

> *"The Only Person You Are Destined*
> *To Become Is*
> *The Person You Decide To Be."*
>
> *-Ralph Waldo Emerson*

> *"People With Goals Succeed Because*
> *They Know Where They Are Going...*
> *It's As Simple As That."*
>
> *-Earl Nightingale*

Is Real Estate Sales right for you? In previous chapters, I have written what I know it takes to become a real estate sales agent/REALTOR® *and* what makes a successful REALTOR®. Those who belong in real estate are those who sincerely want to help people. They are willing to put in the time necessary to learn from professionals already in the business. They focus on what is best for their clients and they develop excellent time management skills so they can have a fulfilling life with their spouse and kids, time for recreation, self-fulfillment, and satisfaction as well as selling real estate. They know it is a sales position/profession, and they do what it takes to find buyers and sellers who are ready, willing and able to work with them without wasting their time on people who do not qualify as clients.

They are constantly educating and re-educating themselves. They know what to say, how to say it, and when to say it in every phase of the business. They are "EXPERTS."

It takes a lot of learning, coaching and experience to make it. But with the right attitude and right mentor, you won't have to learn many of those lessons the hard way as I did.

I believe that in this book I have given you the best possible advice learned from my own hard-earned experiences, the many books I have read and the innumerable seminars attended throughout my life.

It hurts when you forget to make sure you have the second decision maker with you at your first appointment with that prospective client and that person decides to buy or list with another agent even after you spent hours and hours with them. You can feel betrayed and really hurt and discouraged. It also hurts when you really never asked their motivation on a scale of one to ten and find out after months of showing property that they really had motivation of only three and never bought. You waste gas, time away from home, time with the kids, even perhaps during the holidays. All is lost because you did not fully qualify your prospective buyers or sellers as outlined in this book. It is a waste which leads to aborting what could have been a promising and successful career.

If real estate is to become your career, you need to commit to systems, discipline, focus and education to learn what to do, how to do it, why to do it and when to do it. You must know what to say, when to say it, and how to say it with your heart and soul, as you help your clients accomplish what they expect you to help them accomplish.

You also MUST be an optimist, and you MUST be the strong and disciplined one when emotions and trials occur. (An airplane engine catches fire, or the weather gets bad along the way.) Optimism, knowledge and ability of an EXPERT are an absolute necessity. You will know there is a way when it doesn't look good. You focus on the positive and on accomplishing your client's goal. You will be the calm in the middle of the storm.

Your heart will be warmed every time you help them get that home or property of their dreams because of your expertise. You will find they are your new friends, and during your career you will see families develop and grow. You will also continue to be rewarded as you continue to be involved in their lives. It is truly a life worth living!

Just remember it is a *people* business in which you, having become an EXPERT, have the opportunity to serve people and families, and you will be rewarded in more ways than you could ever dream possible.

I sincerely hope that I have helped you to see what this profession requires and have saved you from a great deal of frustration that invariably comes from trying to do something that just does not fit who you are. At the same time, I hope I have enlightened and encouraged those of you who are *right* for real estate sales to go forward now that you have time-saving information that, when applied, will aid in your success.

If you are *truly committed* to get to that 4th level of performance where you are unconsciously competent, where you are an EXPERT with all the skills of a truly professional real estate agent/REALTOR®, then I encourage you to GO FORWARD!

As a final reminder, the Real Estate systems mentioned in this book can give you a life worth living. Without them you are not in control. You may make a lot of money but not have much of a life. You have a lot to learn!! Now, just DO IT!

Is Real Estate Sales Right For You?

> *The Most Beautiful Satisfaction*
> *In The World*
> *Is When Someone Appreciates*
> *Your Work.*

> *"I've Learned That People Will Forget What You Said, People Will Forget What You Did, But People Will Never Forget How You Made Them Feel."*
>
> *-Maya Angelou*

More About The Author

Here is what he believes contributed to his success: Joe was born in Denver, Colorado. He moved with his parents to Los Angeles, California as a result of World War II. At age six he moved with his parents to a small town in North Dakota. During the next five years until age eleven, he traveled each summer with his family back to Grandma's home in Los Angeles where his father was working on his PhD at the University of Southern California. Soon afterwards, the family relocated permanently to Los Angeles where Joe attended Middle School and High School before graduating from the University of Southern California Riverside. These several moves and travels throughout a considerable portion of the country during his early life exposed Joe to not only numerous climates and environments but to considerable cultural diversity as well. And though he did not realize it at the time, these early moves actually paved the way to his eventual interest in real estate. They also instilled within him considerable empathy with others, adults *and children*, who are sometimes required to move to new and different locations.

After college and a couple of different sales and management positions, Joe found himself in San Diego, and in 1975 he began his focus entirely on real estate sales. After obtaining his real estate sales license, he continued to attend all of the related seminars and courses he could find including achieving his Graduate of REALTORS® Institute (GRI) designation in 1977 and his Broker's license in 1978. Thus, for more than 39 years, Joe's career has focused exclusively on, and

More About the Author

included, virtually every facet of real estate sales from investment and commercial to residential and even business sales that involved real estate. As his career developed, he sometimes regretted that he did not have a personal mentor to coach and advise him, and as a result, he was often forced to learn things on his own – sometimes the "hard way." That is one of the reasons that compelled him to write this book.

Today Joe and his second wife Paula, who holds the National Association Of REALTORS® designations of CRS, GRI and SRES, Senior Residential Specialist, continue to live in the San Diego area where they own and operate their firm, Realty Experts, with several offices and over 80 real estate agents and brokers. Only 3% of all agents in the country hold the designation Certified Residential Specialist (CRS)

For those who qualify, Joe provides training, coaching, mentoring and counseling services. Through their firm's Training Academy, they provide in-depth training for sales agent licensing and preparation for a successful career in real estate.

You can reach Joe at 858-967-8801 by calling or texting or email him at JoeCobb@RealtyExperts.Net. He is also on Facebook and LinkedIn. He would love to meet you and encourage you in your career.

www.ingramcontent.com/pod-product-compliance
Lightning Source LLC
Chambersburg PA
CBHW051724170526
45167CB00002B/785